CALIFORNIA,
ROMANTIC AND RESOURCEFUL

CALIFORNIA, ROMANTIC AND RESOURCEFUL

JOHN FRANCIS DAVIS

ISBN: 978-93-5614-577-1

Published: 1914

LECTOR HOUSE LLP
E-MAIL: info@lectorhouse.com

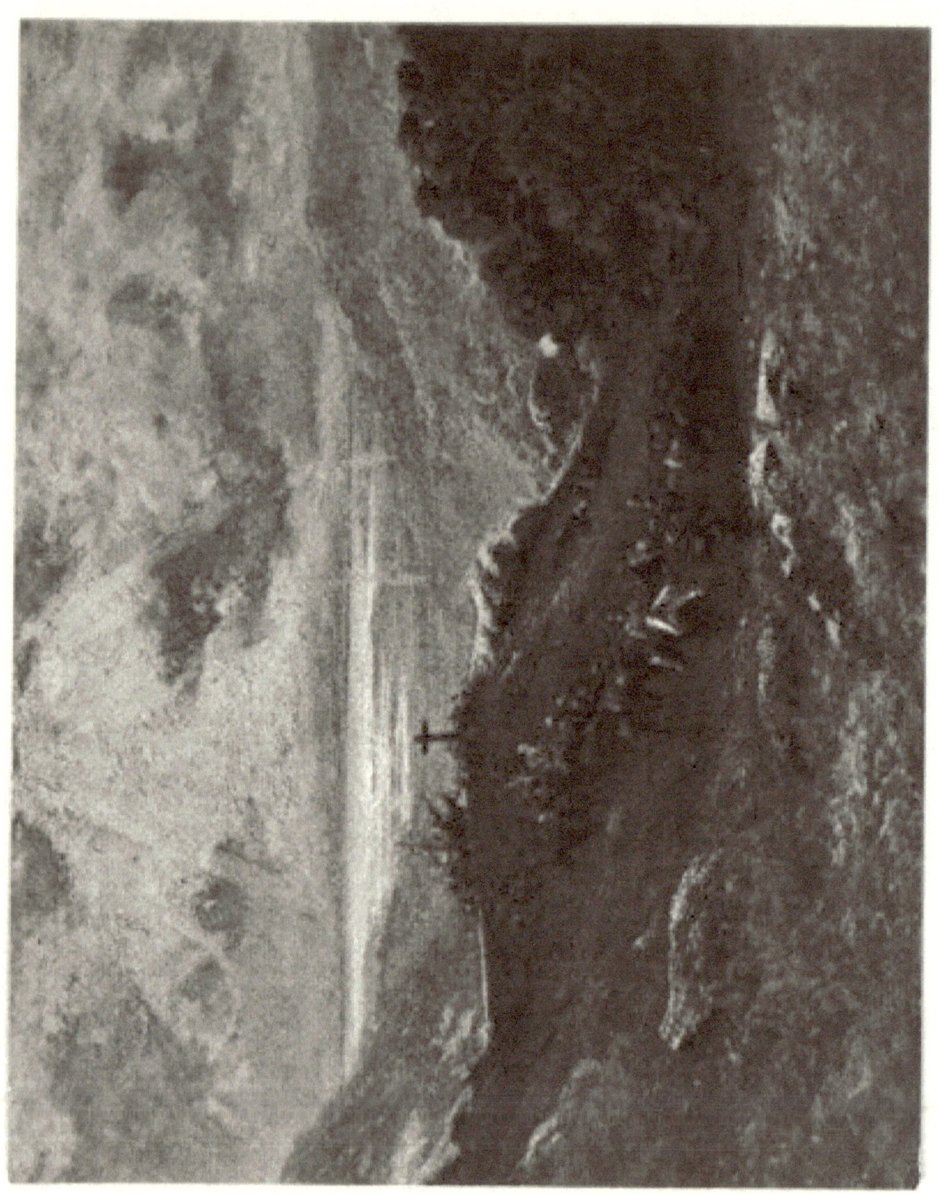

DISCOVERY OF SAN FRANCISCO BAY BY PORTOLÁ

From the oil painting by William Keith, in the possession of
Mrs. Phoebe A. Hearst, at Hacienda del Pozo de Verona, Cal.

CALIFORNIA,
ROMANTIC AND RESOURCEFUL

A PLEA FOR THE COLLECTION
PRESERVATION AND DIFFUSION
OF INFORMATION RELATING
TO PACIFIC COAST HISTORY

BY

JOHN F. DAVIS

The Californian loves his state because his state loves him. He returns her love with a fierce affection that to men who do not know California is always a surprise.—DAVID STARR JORDAN in *"California and the Californians."*

As we transmit our institutions, so we shall transmit our blood and our names to future ages and populations. What altitudes shall throng these shores, what cities shall gem the borders of the sea! Here all peoples and all tongues shall meet. Here shall be a more perfect civilization, a more thorough intellectual development, a firmer faith, a more reverent worship. Perhaps, as we look back to the struggle of an earlier age, and mark the steps of our ancestors in the career we have traced, some thoughtful man of letters in ages yet to come may bring light the history of this shore or of this day. I am sure, Ludlow citizens, that whoever shall hereafter read it will perceive that our pride and joy are dimmed by no stain of selfishness. Our pride is for humanity; our joy is for the world; and amid all the wonders of past achievement and all the splendors of present success, we turn with swelling hearts to gaze into the boundless future, with the earnest conviction that will develop a universal brotherhood of man.

—E. D. Baker, Atlantic Cable Address.

TO
CHARLES STETSON WHEELER
An Able Advocate
A Good Citizen, A Devoted Husband and Father
A Loyal Friend
This Little Book is
Affectionately Dedicated

PREFACE

This plea is an arrow shot into the air. It is the result of an address which I made at Colton Hall, in Monterey, upon the celebration of Admission Day, 1908, and another which I made at a luncheon meeting of the Commonwealth Club, at the Palace Hotel, San Francisco, on April 12, 1913. These addresses have been amplified and revised, and certain statistics contained in them have been brought down to the end of 1913. In this form they go forth to a larger audience, in the earnest hope that they may meet a kind reception, and somewhere find a generous friend.

The subject of Pacific Coast history is one of surpassing interest to Californians. Some fine additions to our store of knowledge have been made of late years, notably the treatise of Zoeth S. Eldredge on "The Beginnings of San Francisco," published by the author, in San Francisco, in 1912; the treatise of Irving Berdine Richman on "California under Spain and Mexico, 1535-1847," published by the Houghton Mifflin Company, of Boston and New York, in 1911; the warm appreciation of E. D. Baker, by Elijah R. Kennedy, entitled "The Contest for California in 1861," published by the Houghton Mifflin Company, in Boston and New York, in 1912; the monumental work on "Missions and Missionaries of California," by Fr. Zephyrin Engelhardt, published by the James H. Barry Company, of San Francisco, 1908-1913, and the "Guide to Materials for the History of the United States in the Principal Archives of Mexico," by Herbert E. Bolton, Ph. D., Professor of American History in the University of California, the publication of which by the Carnegie Institution of Washington, at Washington, D. C., in 1913, is an event of epochal historical importance. All of these works and the recent activities in Spain of Charles E. Chapman, the Traveling Fellow of the University of California, the publications of the Academy of Pacific Coast History, at Berkeley, edited by F. J. Teggart, and the forthcoming publication at San Francisco of "A Bibliography of California and the Pacific West," by Robert Ernest Cowan, only emphasize the importance of original research work in Pacific Coast history, and the necessity for prompt action to preserve the remaining sources of its romantic and inspiring story.

JOHN F. DAVIS.

San Francisco, July 1, 1914.

CONTENTS

LIST OF ILLUSTRATIONS

CALIFORNIA,
ROMANTIC AND RESOURCEFUL

One of the most important acts of the Grand Parlor of the Native Sons of the Golden West which met at Lake Tahoe in 1910 was the appropriation of approximately fifteen hundred dollars for the creation of a traveling fellowship in Pacific Coast history at the State University. In pursuance of the resolution adopted, a committee of five was appointed by the head of the order to confer with the authorities of the university in the matter of this fellowship. The university authorities were duly notified, both of the appropriation for the creation of the fellowship and of the appointment of the committee, and the plan was put into practical operation. In 1911 this action was reaffirmed, and a resident fellowship was also created, making an appropriation of three thousand dollars, which has been repeated each year since. Henry Morse Stephens, Sather Professor of History, and Herbert E. Bolton, Professor of American History, and their able assistants in the history department of the university have hailed with delight this public-spirited movement on the part of that organization.

The object and design of these fellowships is to aid in the collection, preservation and publication of information and material relating to the history of the Pacific Coast. Archives at Querétaro and Mexico City, in Mexico, at Seville, Simancas and Madrid, in Spain, and in Paris, London and St. Petersburg are veritable treasure mines of information concerning our early Pacific Coast history, and the correspondence of many an old family and the living memory of many an individual pioneer can still furnish priceless records of a later period. Professor Stephens has elaborated a practical scheme for making available all these sources of historical information through the providence of these fellowships, as far as they reach.

The perpetuation of these traditions, the preservation of this history, is of the highest importance. Five years ago, at Monterey, upon the celebration of the anniversary of Admission Day, I took occasion to urge this view, and I have not ceased to urge it ever since. If we take any pride in our State, if the tendrils of affection sink into the soil where our fathers wrought, and where we ourselves abide and shall leave sons and daughters after us, if we know and feel any appreciation of local color, or take any interest in the drama of life that is being enacted on these Western shores, then the preservation of every shred of it is of vital importance to us—at least as Californians.

The early history of this coast came as an offshoot of a civilization whose antiquity was already respectable. "A hundred years before John Smith saw the spot on which was planted Jamestown," says Hubert H. Bancroft, "thousands from

Spain had crossed the high seas, achieving mighty conquests, seizing large portions of the two Americas and placing under tribute their peoples."

CARMEL MISSION, NEAR MONTEREY,
WHERE JUNÍPERO SERRA IS BURIED.

The past of California possesses a wealth of romantic interest, a variety of contrast, a novelty of resourcefulness and an intrinsic importance that enthralls the imagination. I shall not attempt to speak of the hardship and high endeavor of the splendid band of navigators, beginning with Cabrillo in 1542, who discovered, explored and reported on its bays, outlets, rivers and coast line; whose exploits were as heroic as anything accomplished by the Norsemen in Iceland, or the circumnavigators of the Cape of Good Hope. I do not desire to picture the decades of the pastoral life of the hacienda and its broad acres, that culminated in "the splendid idle forties." I do not intend to recall the miniature struggles of Church and State, the many political controversies of the Mexican regime, or the play of plot and counterplot that made up so much of its history "before the Gringo came." I shall not try to tell the story of the discovery of gold and its world-thrilling incidents, nor of the hardships and courage of the emigrant trail, nor of the importance of the mission of the Pathfinder, and the excitement of the conquest, each in itself an experience that full to the brim.

Let me rather call attention to three incidents of our history, ignoring all the rest, to enforce the point of its uniqueness, its variety, its novelty, its importance, as entitling it to its proper proportionate place in the history of the nation.

And first of all, the story of the missions. The story of the missions is the history of the beginning of the colonization of California. The Spanish Government was desirous of providing its ships, on the return trip from Manila, with good harbors of supply and repairs, and was also desirous of promoting a settlement of the north as a safeguard against possible Russian aggression. The Franciscans, upon the expulsion of the Jesuits in 1767, had taken charge of the missions, and, in their zeal for the conversion of the Indians, seconded the plans of the government.

"The official purpose here, as in older mission undertakings," says Dr. Josiah Royce, "was a union of physical and spiritual conquest, soldiers under a military governor co-operating to this end with missionaries and mission establishments. The natives were to be overcome by arms in so far as they might resist the conquerors, were to be attracted to the missions by peaceable measures in so far as might prove possible, were to be instructed in the faith, and were to be kept for the present under the paternal rule of the clergy, until such time as they might be ready for a free life as Christian subjects. Meanwhile, Spanish colonists were to be brought to the new land as circumstances might determine, and, to these, allotments of land were to be made. No grants of lands, in a legal sense, were made or promised to the mission establishments, whose position was to be merely that of spiritual institutions, intrusted with the education of neophytes, and with the care of the property that should be given or hereafter produced for the purpose. On the other hand, if the government tended to regard the missions as purely subsidiary to its purpose, the outgoing missionaries to this strange land were so much the more certain to be quite uncorrupted by worldly ambitions, by a hope of acquiring wealth, or by any intention to found a powerful ecclesiastical government in the new colony. They went to save souls, and their motive was as single as it was worthy of reverence. In the sequel, the more successful missions of Upper California became, for a time, very wealthy; but this was only by virtue of the gifts of nature and of the devoted labors of the padres."

Such a scheme of human effort is so unique, and so in contradiction to much that obtains today, that it seems like a narrative from another world. Fortunately, the annals of these missions, which ultimately extended from San Diego to beyond Sonoma—stepping-stones of civilization on this coast—are complete, and their simple disinterestedness and directness sound like a tale from Arcady. They were signally successful because those who conducted them were true to the trustee-ship of their lives. They cannot be held responsible if they were unable in a single generation to eradicate in the Indian the ingrained heredity of shiftlessness of all the generations that had gone before. It is a source of high satisfaction that there was on the part of the padres no record of overreaching the simple native, no failure to respect what rights they claimed, no carnage and bloodshed, that have so often attended expeditions sent nominally for civilization, but really for conquest. Here, at least, was one record of missionary endeavor that came to full fruition and flower, and knew no fear or despair, until it attracted the attention of the ruthless rapacity and greed of the Mexican governmental authority crouching behind the project of secularization. The enforced withdrawal of the paternal hand before the Indian had learned to stand and walk alone, coupled in some sections with the dread scourge of pestilential epidemic, wrought dispersion, decimation and destruction. If, however, the teeming acres are now otherwise tilled, and if the herds of cattle have passed away and the communal life is gone forever, the record of what was accomplished in those pastoral days has linked the name of California with a new and imperishable architecture, and has immortalized the name of Junípero Serra[1]. The pathetic ruin at Carmel is a shattered monument above a grave that will become a world's shrine of pilgrimage in honor of one of humanity's heroes. The patient soul that here laid down its burden will not be forgotten. The memory of the brave heart that was here consumed with love for mankind will live through the ages. And, in a sense, the work of these missions is not dead—their very ruins still preach the lesson of service and of sacrifice. As the fishermen off the coast of Brittany tell the legend that at the evening hour, as their boats pass over the vanished Atlantis, they can still hear the sounds of its activity at the bottom of the sea, so every Californian, as he turns the pages of the early history of his State, feels at times that he can hear the echo of the Angelus bells of the missions, and amid the din of the money-madness of these latter days, can find a response in "the better angels of his nature."

In swift contrast to this idyllic scene, which is shared with us by few other sections of this country, stands the history of a period where for nearly two years this State was without authority of American civil law, and where, in practice, the only authority was such as sprang from the instinct of self-preservation. No more interesting phase of history in America can be presented than that which arose in California immediately after the discovery of gold, with reference to titles upon the public domain. James W. Marshall made the discovery of gold in the race of a small mill at Coloma, in the latter part of January, 1848. Thereupon took place an incident of history which demonstrated that Jason and his companions were not

---

[1] Pronounced Hoo-neep-ero, with the accent on the second syllable.

the only Argonauts who ever made a voyage to unknown shores in search of a golden fleece. The first news of the discovery almost depopulated the towns and ranches of California, and even affected the discipline of the small army of occupation. The first winter brought thousands of Oregonians, Mexicans and Chilenos. The extraordinary reports that reached the East were at first disbelieved, but when the private letters of army officers and men in authority were published, an indescribable gold fever took possession of the nation east of the Alleghanies. All the energetic and daring, all the physically sound of all ages, seemed bent on reaching the new El Dorado. "The old Gothic instinct of invasion seemed to survive and thrill in the fiber of our people," and the camps and gulches and mines of California witnessed a social and political phenomenon unique in the history of the world—the spirit and romance of which have been immortalized in the pages of Bret Harte.

Before 1850 the population of California had risen from 15,000, as it was in 1847[2], to 100,000, and the average weekly increase for six weeks thereafter was 50,000. The novelty of this situation produced in many minds the most marvelous development. "Every glance westward was met by a new ray of intelligence; every drawn breath of western air brought inspiration; every step taken was over an unknown field; every experiment, every thought, every aspiration and act were original and individual."

At the time of Marshall's discovery, the United States was still at war with Mexico, its sovereignty over the soil of California not being recognized by the latter. The treaty of Guadalupe Hidalgo was not signed until February 2d, and the ratified copies thereof not exchanged at Querétaro till May 30, 1848. On the 12th of February, 1848, ten days after the signing of the treaty of peace and about three weeks after the discovery of gold at Coloma, Colonel Mason did the pioneers a signal service by issuing, as Governor, the proclamation concerning the mines, which at the time was taken as a finality and certainty as to the status of mining titles in

---

[2] The best pen-picture of San Francisco just before the discovery of gold that I know of is that given by one who was an eye-witness: "At that time (July, 1847), what is now called San Francisco was called Yerba Buena. A naval officer, Lieutenant Washington A. Bartlett, its first Alcalde, had caused it to be surveyed and laid out into blocks and lots, which were being sold at sixteen dollars a lot of fifty varas square; the understanding being that no single person could purchase of the Alcalde more than one in-lot of fifty varas, and one out-lot of a hundred varas. Folsom, however, got his clerks, orderlies, etc., to buy lots, and they, for a small consideration, conveyed them to him, so that he was nominally the owner of a good many lots. Lieutenant Halleck had bought one of each kind, and so had Warner. Many naval officers had also invested, and Captain Folsom advised me to buy some, but I felt actually insulted that he should think me such a fool as to pay money for property in such a horrid place as Yerba Buena, especially in his quarter of the city, then called Happy Valley. At that day Montgomery Street was, as now, the business street, extending from Jackson to Sacramento, the water of the bay leaving barely room for a few houses on its east side, and the public warehouses were on a sandy beach about where the Bank of California now stands, viz., near the intersection of Sansome and California streets . . . . The population was estimated at about four hundred, of whom Kanakas (natives of the Sandwich Islands) formed the bulk."—Personal Memoirs of General W. T. Sherman (Charles L. Webster & Co., New York, 1891), p. 61.

their international aspect. "From and after this date," the proclamation read, "the Mexican laws and customs now prevailing in California relative to the denouncement of mines are hereby abolished." Although, as the law was fourteen years afterwards expounded by the United States Supreme Court, the act was unnecessary as a precautionary measure[3] still the practical result of the timeliness of the proclamation was to prevent attempts to found private titles to the new discovery of gold on any customs or laws of Mexico.

Meantime, California was governed by military authority,—was treated as if it were merely a military outpost, away out somewhere west of the "Great American Desert." Except an act to provide for the deliveries and taking of mails at certain points on the coast, and a resolution authorizing the furnishing of arms and ammunition to certain immigrants, no Federal act was passed with reference to California in any relation; in no act of Congress was California even mentioned after its annexation, until the act of March 3, 1849, extending the revenue laws of the United States "over the territory and waters of Upper California, and to create certain collection districts therein." This act of March 3, 1849, not only did not extend the general laws of the United States over California, but did not even create a local tribunal for its enforcement, providing that the District Court of Louisiana and the Supreme Court of Oregon should be courts of original jurisdiction to take cognizance of all violations of its provisions. Not even the act of September 9, 1850, admitting California into the Union, extended the general laws of the United States over the State by express provision. Not until the act of September 26, 1850, establishing a District Court in the State, was it enacted by Congress "that all the laws of the United States which are not locally inapplicable shall have the same force and effect within the said State of California as elsewhere in the United States[4]."

---

[3] *United States* vs. *Castellero*, 2 Black (67 U. S.), 17-371.

[4] A vivid and most interesting account of General Sutter's helpless attempt to obtain from the military Governor a recognition of his title to the land upon which his tail race was situated is given by General W. T. Sherman: "I remember one day in the spring of 1848, that two men, Americans, came into the office and inquired for the Governor. I asked their business, and one answered that they had just come down from General Sutter on special business, and wanted to see Governor Mason *in person*. I took them in to the Colonel, and left them together. After sometime the Colonel came to his door and called to me. I went in, and my attention was directed to a series of papers unfolded on his table, in which lay about half an ounce of *placer* gold . . . . Colonel Mason then handed me a letter from Captain Sutter, addressed to him, stating that he (Sutter) was engaged in erecting a sawmill at Coloma, about forty miles up the American Fork, above his fort at New Helvetia, for the general benefit of the settlers in that vicinity; that he had incurred considerable expense, and wanted a 'preëmption' to the quarter section of land on which the mill was located, embracing the tail-race in which this particular gold had been found. Mason instructed me to prepare a letter, reciting that California was yet a Mexican province, simply held by us as a conquest; that no laws of the United States yet applied to it, much less the land laws or preëmption laws, which could only apply after a public survey. Therefore it was impossible for the Governor to promise him (Sutter) a title to the land; yet, as there were no settlements within forty miles, he was not likely to be disturbed by trespassers. Colonel Mason signed the letter, handed it to one of the gentlemen who had brought the sample of gold, and they departed . . . . That gold was the *first* discovered in the Sierra Nevada, which soon rev-

SUTTER'S MILL AT COLOMA

A reproduction of photograph in possession of Charles B. Turrill, of San Francisco, from original daguerreotype taken on the spot by R. H. Vance in 1850. James W. Marshall in the foreground.

Though no general Federal laws were extended by Congress over the later

olutionized the whole country, and actually moved the whole civilized world." —Personal Memoirs, p. 68.

acquisitions from Mexico for more than two years after the end of the war, the paramount title to the public lands had vested in the Federal Government by virtue of the provisions of the treaty of peace; the public land itself had become part of the public domain of the United States. The army of occupation, however, offered no opposition to the invading army of prospectors. The miners were, in 1849, twenty years ahead of the railroad and the electric telegraph. The telephone had not yet been invented. In the parlance of the times, the prospectors "had the drop" on the army. In Colonel Mason's unique report of the situation that confronted him, discretion waited upon valor. "The entire gold district," he wrote to the Government at Washington, "with few exceptions of grants made some years ago by the Mexican authorities, is on land belonging to the United States. It was a matter of serious reflection with me how I could secure to the Government certain rents or fees for the privilege of procuring this gold; but upon considering the large extent of the country, *the character of the people engaged, and the small scattered force at my command*, I am resolved not to interfere, but permit all to work freely." It is not recorded whether the resolute colonel was conscious of the humor of his resolution. This early suggestion of conservation was, under the circumstances, manifestly academic.

The Supreme Court of the United States, in commenting on the singular situation in which Colonel Mason found himself, clearly and forcefully states his predicament. "*His position*," says that Court, "*was unlike anything that had preceded it in the history of our country* . . . . It was not without its difficulties, both as regards the principle upon which he should act, and the actual state of affairs in California. He knew that the Mexican inhabitants of it had been remitted by the treaty of peace to those municipal laws and usages which prevailed among them before the territory had been ceded to the United States, but that a state of things and population had grown up during the war, and after the treaty of peace, which made some other authority necessary to maintain the rights of the ceded inhabitants and of immigrants, from misrule and violence. He may not have comprehended fully the principle applicable to what he might rightly do in such a case, but he felt rightly and acted accordingly. He determined, in the absence of all instruction, to maintain the existing government. The territory had been ceded as a conquest, and was to be preserved and governed as such until the sovereignty to which it had passed had legislated for it. That sovereignty was the United States, under the Constitution, by which power had been given to Congress to dispose of and make all needful rules and regulations respecting the territory or other property belonging to the United States, with the power also to admit new states into this Union, with only such limitations as are expressed in the section in which this power is given. The government, of which Colonel Mason was the executive, had its origin in the lawful exercise of a belligerent right over a conquered territory. It had been instituted during the war by the command of the President of the United States. It was the government when the territory was ceded as a conquest, and it did not cease, as a matter of course, or as a necessary consequence of the restoration of peace. The President might have dissolved it by withdrawing the army and navy officers who administered it, but he did not do so. Congress could have put an end to it, but that was not done. The right inference from the inaction of both is, that it was meant to be continued until it had been legislatively changed. No presumption of a contrary intention can be made. Whatever may have been the causes of delay, it must be presumed that the delay was consistent with the true policy of the Government[5]."

This guess, being the last guess, must now be taken as authoritative.

The prospectors and miners were, then, in the start, simply trespassers upon the public lands as against the Government of the United States, with no laws to guide, restrain or protect them, and with nothing to fear from the military authorities. They were equal to the occasion. The instinct of organization was a part of their heredity. Professor Macy, in a treatise issued by Johns Hopkins University, once wrote: "It has been said that if three Americans meet to talk over an item of business, the first thing they do is to organize."

"Finding themselves far from the legal traditions and restraints of the settled East," said the report of the Public Land Commission of 1880, "in a pathless wilderness, under the feverish excitement of an industry as swift and full of chance as the throwing of dice, the adventurers of 1849 spontaneously instituted neighborhood or district codes of regulation, which were simply meant to define and protect a brief possessory ownership. The ravines and river bars which held the placer gold were valueless for settlement or home-making, but were splendid stakes to hold for a few short seasons and gamble with nature for wealth or ruin.

"In the absence of State and Federal laws competent to meet the novel industry, and with the inbred respect for equitable adjustments of rights between man and man, the miners sought only to secure equitable rights and protection from robbery by a simple agreement as to the maximum size of a surface claim, trusting, with a well-founded confidence, that no machinery was necessary to enforce their regulations other than the swift, rough blows of public opinion. The gold-seekers were not long in realizing that the source of the dust which had worked its way into the sands and bars, and distributed its precious particles over the bedrocks of rivers was derived from solid quartz veins, which were thin sheets of mineral material inclosed in the foundation rocks of the country. Still in advance of any enactments by legislature or Congress, the common sense of the miners, which had proved strong enough to govern with wisdom the ownership of placer mines, rose to meet the question of lode claims and sheet-like veins of quartz, and provided that a claim should consist of a certain horizontal block of the vein, however it might run, but extending indefinitely downward, with a strip of surface on, or embracing the vein's outcrop, for the placing of necessary machinery and buildings. Under this theory, the lode was the property, and the surface became a mere easement.

"This early California theory of a mining claim, consisting of a certain number of running feet of vein, with a strip of land covering the surface length of the claim, is, the obvious foundation for the Federal legislation and present system of public disposition and private ownership of the mineral lands west of the Missouri River. Contrasted with this is the mode of disposition of mineral-bearing lands east of the Missouri River, where the common law has been the rule, and where the surface

---

[5] *Cross* vs. *Harrison*, 16 Howard (57 U. S.), 164, 192.

tract has always carried with it all minerals vertically below it.

"The great coal, copper, lead and zinc wealth east of the Rocky Mountains has all passed with the surface titles, and there can be little doubt if California had been contiguous to the eastern metallic regions, and its mineral development progressed naturally with the advantage of homemaking settlements, the power of common-law precedent would have governed its whole mining history. But California was one of these extraordinary historic exceptions that defy precedent and create original modes of life and law. And since the developers of the great precious metal mining of the Far West have, for the most part, swarmed out of the California hive, California ideas have not only been everywhere dominant over the field of the industry, but have stemmed the tide of Federal land policy, and given us a statute-book with English common law in force over half the land and California common law ruling in the other."

I have spoken of these two incidents, the one of the peaceable civilization of the missions, and the other of the strenuous life issuing in the adoption of the mining law, as illustrative incidents of the variety of California history. Let me briefly speak of a third one, California's method of getting into the Union. But two other states at the present time celebrate the anniversary of their admission into the Union; the reason for California's celebration of that anniversary is well founded. The delay incident to the admission of California into the Union as a State was precipitated by the tense struggle then raging in Congress between the North and the South. The admission of Wisconsin had made a tie, fifteen free states and fifteen slave states. The destiny of the nation hung upon the result of that issue, and when California finally entered the Union, it came in as the sixteenth free State, forever destroyed the equilibrium between the North and the South, and made the Civil War practically inevitable. The debate was a battle of giants. Webster, Clay and Calhoun all took part in it. Calhoun had arisen from his death-bed to fight the admission of California, and, upon reaching his seat in the Senate, found himself so overcome with weakness and pain that he had Mason of Virginia read the speech he had prepared in writing. Webster atoned for his hostility to the Pacific Coast before the Mexican War by answering Calhoun. "I do not hesitate to avow in the presence of the living God that if you seek to drive us from California . . . I am for disunion," declared Robert Toombs, of Georgia, to an applauding House. "The unity of our empire hangs upon the decision of this day," answered Seward in the Senate. National history was being made with a vengeance, and California was the theme. The contest was an inspiring one, and a reading of the Congressional Record covering the period makes a Californian's blood tingle with the intensity of it all[6].

The struggle had been so prolonged, however, that the people upon this coast,

[6] "In 1850 the Congress of the United States passed what is called a series of compromise measures. Among them was a fugitive slave law, the indemnity to Texas, the creation of territories in Utah and New Mexico, the admission of California, and the change in the Texas boundary. Four of them had direct relation to the question of slavery, and one was the admission of this State. Being in Congress, as a member of the House, at that time, I know well what you remember. The admission of California as a State was delayed for some nine or ten months, because the leaders of the Pro-Slavery Party were determined to secure their

far removed from the scene of it, and feeling more than all else that they were entitled to be protected by a system of laws, had grown impatient. They had finally proceeded in a characteristically Californian way. They had met in legislative assembly and proclaimed: "It is the duty of the Government of the United States to give us laws; and when that duty is not performed, one of the clearest rights we have left is to govern ourselves."

The first provisional government meeting was held in the pueblo of San Jose, December 11, 1848, and unanimously recommended that a general convention be held at the pueblo of San Jose on the second Monday of January following. At San Francisco a similar provisional meeting was held, though the date of the proposed convention was fixed for the first Monday in March, 1849, and afterward changed to the first Monday in August.

The various assemblies which had placed other conditions and fixed other dates and places for holding the same gave way, and a general election was finally held under the provisions of a proclamation issued by General Bennet Riley, the United States General commanding, a proclamation for the issuance of which there was no legislative warrant whatever. While the Legislative Assembly of San Francisco recognized his military authority, in which capacity he was not formidable, it did not recognize his civil power. General Riley, however, with that rare diplomacy which seems to have attached to all Federal military people when acting on the Pacific Coast, realizing that any organized government that proceeded from an orderly concourse of the people was preferable to the exasperating condition in which the community was left to face its increasing problem under Congressional inaction, himself issued the proclamation for a general convention, which is itself a gem. The delegates met in Monterey, at Colton Hall, on the 1st of September, and organized on the 3d of September, 1849.

The convention was one of the keenest and most intelligent that ever assembled for the fulfillment of a legislative responsibility. Six of the delegates had resided in California less than six months, while only twenty-one, exclusive of the seven native Californians, had resided here for more than three years. The average age of all the delegates was 36 years. The debates of that convention should be familiar to every citizen of this State. No Californian should be unfamiliar with the great debate on what was to constitute the eastern boundary of the State of California, a debate accompanied by an intensity of feeling which in the end almost wrecked the convention. The dramatic scenes wrought by the patriotism that saved the wrecking of the convention stand out in bold relief. The constitution adopted by this convention was ratified November 13, 1849, and, at the same election, an entire State and legislative ticket, with two representatives in Congress, was chosen. The senators and assemblymen elect met in San Jose on December 15, 1849. On December 20, 1849, the *State government* of California was established and Governor Peter H. Burnett was inaugurated as the first Governor of the State of California, and soon thereafter William M. Gwin and John C. Frémont were elected the first United States Senators of the *State of California*. Notwithstanding the

own way on all the other measures before California should be admitted." — E. D. BAKER, Forest Hill speech, Aug. 19, 1859.

fact that there had never been any territorial form of government, notwithstanding the fact that California had not yet been admitted into the Union, these men were all elected as members of the *State government*, and the United States Senators and members of Congress started for Washington to help get the State admitted.

OLD COLTON HALL AND JAIL, MONTEREY

Immediately upon the inauguration of Governor Burnett, General Riley issued this remarkable proclamation:

"To the People of California: A new executive having been elected and installed into office, in accordance with the provisions of the Constitution of the State, the undersigned hereby resigns his powers as Governor of California. In thus dissolving his official connection with the people of this country he would tender to them his heart-felt thanks for their many kind attentions and for the uniform support which they have given to the measures of his administration. The principal object of all his wishes is now accomplished—the people have a government of their own choice, and one which, under the favor of Divine Providence, will secure their own prosperity and happiness and the permanent welfare of *the new State*."

No matter what the legal objections to this course might be, notwithstanding the fact that Congress had as yet passed no bill for the admission of California as a State into the Union, and might never pass one, California broke all precedents by declaring itself a State, and a free State at that, and sent its representatives to Washington to hurry up the passage of the bill which should admit it into the Union.

The brilliant audacity of California's method of admission into the Union stands without parallel in the history of the nation. Outside of the original thirteen colonies, she was the only State carved out of the national domain which was admitted into the Union without a previous enabling act or territorial apprenticeship. What was called the State of Deseret tried it and failed, and the annexation of Texas was the annexation of a foreign republic. The so-called State of Transylvania and State of Franklin had been attempted secessions of western counties of the original states of Virginia and North Carolina, respectively, and their abortive attempts at admission addressed to the Continental Congress, and not to the Congress of the United States. With full right, then, did California, by express resolution spreading the explanation upon the minutes of her constitutional convention[7], avowedly place upon her great seal her Minerva—her "robed goddess-in-arms"—not as the goddess of wisdom, not as the goddess of war, but to signify that as Minerva was not born, but sprang full-armed from the brain of Jupiter, so California, without territorial childhood, sprang full-grown into the sisterhood of states.

When it is remembered that California was not admitted into the Union till September 9, 1850, and yet that the first session of its *State* Legislature had met, legislated, and *adjourned* by April 22, 1850, some appreciation may be had of the speed limit—if there was a limit. The record of the naive self-sufficiency of that Legislature is little short of amazing.

On February 9, 1850, seven months before the admission of the State, it coolly passed the following resolution: "That the Governor be, and he is hereby authorized and requested, to cause to be procured, and prepared in the manner prescribed by the Washington Monument Association, a block of California marble, cinnabar, gold quartz or granite of suitable dimensions, with the word 'California' chiseled on its face, and that he cause the same to be forwarded to the managers of the Washington Monument Association, in the city of Washington, District of Columbia, to constitute a portion of the monument now being erected in that city

[7] J. Ross Browne: Debates in the Convention of California on the Formation of the Constitution in 1849, pp. 304, 322, 323.

to the memory of George Washington." California did not intend to be absent from any feast, or left out of any procession—not if she knew it. Looking back now, our belief is that the only reason she required the word "California," instead of the words "State of California," to be chiseled on the stone was that the rules of the Monument Association probably prohibited any State from chiseling on the stone contributed by it any words except the mere name of the State itself. And the resolution was obeyed—the stone was cut from a marble-bed on a ranch just outside Placerville, and is now in the monument!

On April 13, 1850, nearly five months before California was admitted into the Union, that Legislature gaily passed an act consisting of this provision: "The common law of England, so far as it is not repugnant to or inconsistent with the Constitution of the United States, or the Constitution or laws of the State of California, shall be the rule of the decision in all the courts of the State."

Among other things, three joint resolutions were passed, one demanding of the Federal Government not only a change in the manner of transporting the mails, but also in the manner of their distribution at San Francisco, a second urging upon Congress the importance of authorizing, as soon as practicable, *the construction of a national railroad from the Pacific Ocean to the Mississippi River*—not from the Mississippi River to the Pacific Ocean, but from the Pacific Ocean to the Mississippi River—and a third urging appropriate grants of land by the General Government to each commissioned officer of the Army of the United States who had faithfully and honorably served out a complete term of service in the war with Mexico. Each of the last two resolutions, with grim determination, and without a suspicion of humor, contained this further resolution: "That His Excellency, the Governor, be requested to forward to each of our Senators and Representatives in Congress, a certified copy of this joint resolution."

These resolutions were passed five months before the State was admitted into the Union. If the Senators and Representatives were not yet actually "in Congress"—well, they were at least in Washington—and busy. The desire to be admitted into the Union had developed into a yearning to be considered a part of the Union, had ripened into the conviction that the State was, potentially at least, actually a part of the Union, a yearning and a conviction that became almost pathetic in their intensity. The Legislature adjourned, and for nearly five months the population of San Francisco assembled on the Plaza on the arrival of every Panama steamer, waiting—waiting—waiting for the answer, which, when it did come in the following October, was celebrated with an abandon of joy that has never been equaled on any succeeding Ninth of September.

It is indefensible that in the face of incidents of our history such as these Californians should be ignorant of the lives and experiences of those who preceded them on this coast. The history of their experiences is a part of the history of the nation, and the record of the achievement of the empire-builders of this coast is one that inspires civic pride and a reverence for their memories. Why should the story remain practically unknown? Why should every little unimportant detail of the petty incidents of Queen Anne's War, and King Philip's War, and Braddock's campaign be crammed into the heads of children who until lately never heard the name of Portolá? The beautiful story of Paul Revere's ride is known to everyone, but how many know the story of the invincible determination in the building of Ugarte's ship[8]? William Penn's honest treatment of the Indians is a household word to people who never knew of the existence of Gálvez or Junípero Serra. The story of the hardships of the New England pilgrims in the first winter on the "stern and rock-bound coast" of Massachusetts, is not more pitiful than that of the fate of the immigrants at Donner Lake. The thoughtful magnanimity of Captain Philip of the "Texas" in the moment of victory, in the sea-fight at Santiago, when he checked his men "Don't cheer, boys; the poor fellows are drowning" — is enshrined in the hearts of Americans that never thrilled with pride at Commodore Sloat's solemn and patriotic proclamation upon landing his sailors to hoist the colors at Monterey, a proclamation as fine and dignified as a ritual, that should be committed to memory, as a part of his education, by every schoolboy in California[9]. Longfellow's "Courtship of Miles Standish and Priscilla" is found in every book of declamations, and Bret Harte's poem of the tragic love story of Rezánov and Concha Argüello in complete editions of his works[10]. Why herald the ridiculous attempt of Rhode Island to keep out of the Union, and not acclaim the splendid effort of California to break into it?

The importance to any community of its local history being incorporated in the national story in its proper proportion and perspective cannot be overestimated. When in all the ten volumes of Thomas B. Reed's magnificent collection, entitled "Modern Eloquence," we find but one speech that was delivered in California, and that, while the ancient and admired anecdotage of Chauncey Depew is printed in detail, the flaming eloquence of E. D. Baker is absolutely ignored, and the only discourse reported of Thomas Starr King is one that he delivered in Boston, it is time for the dwellers on these Western shores to ask themselves whether these things have all happened by accident, or whether the older commonwealths of this country have been moved by a pride in their history and in their traditions to take such measures for their preservation and for the promotion of their publication as to put us to shame.

---

[8] The "Triunfo de la Cruz" was begun July 16, 1719, and finally launched at Mulegé, near Loreto, Lower California, on the Feast of the Exaltation of the Cross, Sept. 14, 1719, on its mission to determine whether California was an island, as described and delineated in many official accounts and maps of the period.

[9] The original Proclamation of Commodore Sloat, July 7, 1846, signed by his own hand, here produced, is preserved in Golden Gate Park Museum, San Francisco, to whose Curator, Mr. George Barron, it was recently presented in person as authentic by the lately deceased Rev. S. H. Willey, the chaplain of the Constitutional Convention of 1849 in Colton Hall.

[10] See Appendices A and B.

General Order.

Flag Ship Savannah.
— 7 July 1846.

We are now about to land on the territory of Mexico with whom the U. States is at war. To strike their flag and hoist our own in place of it, is our duty. It is not only our duty to take California, but to preserve it afterwards as a part of the U. States, at all hazards. To accomplish this it is of the first importance to cultivate the good opinions of the inhabitants, and reconcile them to the change. We know how to take care of those who oppose us, but it is the peaceful and unoffending inhabitants whom we must reconcile. I scarcely consider it necessary for me to caution American Seamen and Marines against the detestable crime of plundering and maltreating unoffending inhabitants.

That no one may misunderstand his duty, the following regulations must be strictly adhered to, as no violation can hope to escape the severest punishment.

1st. On landing no man is to leave the Shore until the Commanding Officer gives the order to March.

2nd. No gun is to be fired, or other act of hostility committed without express orders from the Officer Commanding the party.

3rd. The Officers and Boat keepers will keep their respective Boats as close to the Shore as they will safely float taking care they do not lay aground and remain in them prepared to defend themselves against attack, and attentively watch for signals from the ships as well as from the party on shore.

4th. No man is to quit the ranks, or to enter

(any

COMMODORE SLOAT'S GENERAL ORDER

Let me not be misunderstood. I would detract nothing from the glory of other sections of the country. I would minimize nothing of any State's accomplishment. Some of them have a record that is almost a synonym for patriotism. Their tradition is our inheritance; their achievement is our gain. Wisconsin cannot become a veritable workshop of social and economic experiment without the nation being the beneficiary. New England does not enrich her own literature without shedding luster on the literature of the nation. They and theirs belong also to us and to ours. Least of all, do I forget the old Bay State and her high tradition—State of Hancock and Warren, of John Quincy Adams and Webster, of Sumner and Phillips and Garrison and John A. Andrew, of Longfellow and Lowell and Whittier and

Holmes. Her hopes are my hopes; her fears are my fears. May my heart cease its beating if, in any presence or under any pressure, it fail to respond an Amen to the Puritan's prayer: "God save the Commonwealth of Massachusetts."

But if they belong to us, we also belong to them. If their traditions belong to us, so also our tradition belongs to them. We should simply strive that California shall be given her proper proportionate place in the history of the country. We do not find fault with them for having taken the means of heralding abroad their story — we commend them for it. We point to their activity so as to arouse our own people from their amazing inaction. What have we of California done to collect, preserve and diffuse information relating to the history of our State? And what have other commonwealths done?

The California State Historical Society, first organized in 1853, and incorporated in 1876, was in active existence from 1886 to 1894, and published some valuable historical material, including Father Palou's "Noticias," Doyle's "History of the Pious Fund," Willey's "History of the College of California" and some interesting papers of Martin Kellogg, George Davidson, Bernard Moses, William Carey Jones and T. H. Hittell. From that time it has had no active existence. There has not been a meeting of its board of directors since 1893, and since then most of them have died. It has no maps and no manuscripts, and its library of 500 printed volumes was stored away in San Francisco, in the basement cellar of the gentleman who is still nominally its president, until two years ago. It never owned a building in which to do its work, was never endowed, and to all intents and purposes has been dead for twenty years.

When we look beyond the Rockies, however, we begin to appreciate the work that is being done by the State historical societies organized for the purpose of collecting, preserving and diffusing historical information concerning their respective states. The statistics outside California, unless otherwise indicated, are down to 1905. The Massachusetts and Pennsylvania societies are prototypes of the privately organized and endowed organizations of the Eastern states, which, without official patronage, have attained strength, dignity and a high degree of usefulness, while Wisconsin, Minnesota, Iowa and Kansas similarly stand for the State-supported institutions of the West. Twelve societies or departments own their own halls — those valued at $100,000 or over, being Wisconsin, $610,000; Iowa, $400,000; Pennsylvania (1910), $340,000; Massachusetts, $225,000; and Kansas, $200,000. Thirteen are housed in their respective State capitols, seven are quartered in State universities, and six are in other public buildings. The largest State appropriations are: Wisconsin (1910), $31,000; Minnesota, $20,000; and Iowa (1910), $12,000. The Massachusetts, Pennsylvania and Wisconsin societies are, of course, the wealthiest in endowments; possessing, respectively (1912), $420,600, $170,000, and (1910), $63,000 in vested funds. The largest libraries are Pennsylvania (1910), 285,000 titles; Wisconsin (1910), 332,000; Massachusetts (1912), 170,000; Kansas (1910), 191,000; and New Hampshire (1910), 117,500.

Only a little less important in degree are a large number of historical societies which represent some town or section. For example: The Essex Institute of Salem, Massachusetts, with its income of (1913) $15,000, library of 400,000 titles, and building valued at $175,000; New York (City) Historical Society, with 1057 members, endowment fund aggregating $236,000, yearly income of $12,000, and a building costing $400,000; the Chicago Historical Society, with a library of 130,000 titles, housed in a $185,000 building and supported by endowment funds aggregating $111,814; the Long Island Historical Society of Brooklyn, with (1912) 102,500 titles in its own building; the Western Reserve of Cleveland, with 60,000 titles in a $55,000 building; the Worcester (Massachusetts) Society of Antiquities, housing 110,000 titles within a building valued at $50,000; and the Buffalo Historical Society, which has a library of 34,000 titles in a $200,000 building and receives a municipal grant of $5,000 and incidental expenses per annum. These are simply the most highly endowed. Every important town and city in those sections of the country are represented. In the State of Massachusetts alone, there are, besides its State Historical Society, thirty-six local historical societies, all of them alive and active and doing good work. The only historical societies worthy of the name in California, outside of the institution I shall refer to later on, are the Historical Society of Southern California, in Los Angeles, with a membership of fifty, now owning a library of 6,000 titles, housed in the Museum of History, Science and Art in Exposition Park, owned by the county, with the publication of eight volumes of local history to its credit, and the Archeological Institution of the Southwest, also of Los Angeles, the latter institution, however, being not exclusively a historical society.

I submit to you, as Californians, whether this is a record in which we can take any pride. With the exception of the pitiful attempts of its loyal friends from time to time to revive the California Historical Society, absolutely no organization work whatever, except what has lately been initiated at Berkeley, has been done by any public institution to promote the publication of California history or the collection of material therefor. With a history such as ours, with its halo of romance, with its peculiarity of incident, with its epoch-making significance, is it not a burning shame that our people have not long ago, either through private endowment or through public institutions, taken as much pride in the preservation of our history as its makers did in the creation of it? Is it not time that civic societies in every section of this State should combine and work together for the creation of a public sentiment which will support and uphold any institution that will strive to perpetuate the record of the history of this great commonwealth?

Though there has been no sustained or organized effort on the part of the State, or of any community in the State, to recognize the duty of collecting and preserving the priceless records of its historical growth, yet, by the luck that often attends improvidence, we have the nucleus of a library which goes far toward offsetting our culpable indifference.

One of the great fires that swept San Francisco in its early stages just missed the Bancroft Library, then at the corner of Merchant and Montgomery streets. The later fire that burned the building on Market Street, near Third, next door to the History Building, again barely missed the Bancroft Library. And when it was moved to the building especially constructed for it at Valencia and Mission streets, the great conflagration of the 18th of April, 1906, just failed to reach it. In this State it had remained for a private individual, by his life work, to collect and preserve a library that to the State of California is almost priceless in value. This magnificent library the State of California has recently purchased and installed in the California Building, at the State University, where its usefulness is being developed by the Academy of Pacific Coast History, an association organized in connection with the history work of the University. By a series of happy accidents, then, we are in a position to start with as great a nucleus of its historical data as any commonwealth ever had. There remains the great work of cataloguing and publishing, rendering available to the investigation of scholarship this mass of original data, and the State should immediately provide the liberal fund necessary for the mechanical and clerical administrative work.

While the State is completing the trust with reference to the material it already has on hand, the all-destroying march of Time still goes swiftly on, however. Manuscripts in foreign lands are fading and being lost, parchments are becoming moth-eaten or mildewed, whole archives without duplicate are at the mercy of a mob, or a revolution, or a conflagration, and a generation of men and women still alive are quickly passing away, carrying with them an "unsung Iliad" of the Sierras and the plains. In the presence of these facts, we should not stand idle. One great fraternal organization has already done, and is still loyally doing, more than its share. In the great work of endowing fellowships in Pacific Coast history at Berkeley there is room enough for all. Here is an opportunity for private munificence. A fine civism will not find a more pressing necessity, or a more splendid opportunity. An endowment of $100,000 invested in five per cent bonds will yield an annual fellowship fund of $5,000. A citizen looking for an opportunity to do something worth while could find few worthier objects. The fruit of such an endowment may not be as enduring as a noble campanile, or an incomparable Greek theater, yet, in a sense, it will be more lasting than either, for facts become history, and history survives, when campaniles fall and Greek theaters are ground to powder.

It may be that we have not realized that, as it took conscious effort to create the history of the Pacific Coast, it will take conscious effort to see that it is recorded and given its proper place in the history of the country at large. If we have not understood this fact, the recital of the activities of historical societies and other agencies in the East should admonish us that it is time, it has long been time, for us to be up and doing. The record of the history that is now in the making will take care of itself, and the machinery is at hand for its preservation. If we shall become the center of a new culture, be assured that it will be its own press-agent. If we shall see grow into fruition a new music among the redwoods of our Bohemian Grove, there are signs that the world will not be kept ignorant of its origin. Literature reflecting local color will survive as the historic basis for it is known and made secure. The debt we owe to Bret Harte for "The Outcasts of Poker Flat," "The Luck of Roaring Camp," and all the individual types his genius made live again, to Helen Hunt Jackson for her immortal "Ramona," to Charles Fletcher Lummis for his faithful chronicles of splendid pioneering and research, will only be more appreciated as our knowledge of the historic past becomes more accurate and sure.

But it is the record of that very past, the record of our brief, eventful and enthralling past, that concerns us now. Monuments and reminders of it exist on every side. The record also exists, but scattered over the face of the earth, and it has not yet been collected and transcribed. This history cannot be properly taught until it is properly written, and it cannot be properly written until all essential sources shall have been explored. Mines of information are still open that may soon be closed, perhaps forever. Let us promote such action that no element of the grand drama of world-politics once played on these Pacific shores shall be lost. Let us see to it, also, that our fathers' high achievement in a later day shall not be unknown to their descendants. In this cause, let us, with hearts courageous and minds determined, each make good his "full measure of devotion." Thus, may California's story become known of all Americans, and sink into the hearts of a grateful people.

**COMANDANTE'S RESIDENCE, PRESIDIO—
OLDEST ADOBE HOUSE IN SAN FRANCISCO**

APPENDIX A.

THE LOVE-STORY OF CONCHA ARGÜELLO.

[The occasion of the following remarks was the placing of a bronze tablet upon the oldest adobe building in San Francisco, the former residence of the Comandante, now the Officers' Club, at the Presidio, under the auspices of the California Historical Landmarks League, on Serra Day, November 24, 1913. Maria de la Concepción Marcela Argüello (pronounced Arg-wail'-yo), daughter of Don José Dario Argüello, the Comandante of the Presidio, and his wife, Maria Ygnacia Moraga, was born at this Presidio, February 19, 1791 (Original Baptismal Records of Old Mission Dolores, vol. 1, fol. 96, No. 931). The dates of Feb. 26, 1790, given by Bancroft, founded on mere family correspondence, and of Feb. 13, 1791, given by Mary Graham, founded upon a mistaken reading of the baptismal record, are both incorrect. The Spanish pet-name for Concepción (pronounced Con-sep-se-own', with the accent on the last syllable) is Concha (pronounced Cone-cha, the accent strongly on the first syllable, and the cha as in Charles), and its diminutives are Conchita and Conchitita.

Her father was afterward transferred to Santa Barbara, and from there, while he was temporary Governor of California, under the Spanish regime, on Dec. 31, 1814, appointed Governor of Lower California. Her brother, Luis Antonio Argüello, born June 21, 1784, also at the Presidio, died March 27, 1830. He entered the military service as cadet, Sept. 6, 1799; was alférez (ensign), Dec. 23, 1800; lieutenant, March 10, 1806; succeeded his father as Comandante of San Francisco in 1806; was the first Governor of California under Mexican rule, and is buried in the old Mission Dolores cemetery, where the finest monument in the cemetery stands erected to his memory.]

I am glad to see this bronze tablet affixed to this noble adobe building. I take it, that when some of the wooden eye-sores that here abound are torn down, in the necessary beautification that should precede 1915, this old historic building—a monument to Spanish chivalry and hospitality—will be spared. We have too few of them left to lose any of them now. And of all buildings in the world, the Presidio army post should guard this one with jealous care, for here was enacted one of the greatest, sweetest, most tragic love stories of the world—a story which is all the Presidio's own, and which it does not have to share with any other army post.

To you, men of the army, my appeal ought to be an easy one. You have no desire to escape the soft impeachment that the profession of arms has ever been susceptible to the charms of woman. The relation of Mars to Venus is not simply a legend of history, is founded on no mere mythology—their relationship is as sure as the firmament, and their orbits are sometimes very close together.

There is one name that should be the perennial toast of the men of this Presidio. We have just celebrated by a splendid pageant the four-hundredth anniversary of the discovery of the Pacific Ocean by Balboa, and we chose for queen of that ceremony a beautiful girl by the name of Conchita. There was another Conchita once, the daughter of the comandante of this Presidio, the bewitching, the beautiful, the radiant Concha Argüello.

In this old Presidio she was born. In the old Mission Dolores she was christened. Here, it is told, that in the merry exuberance of her innocent babyhood, she danced instead of prayed before the shrine. In the glory of these sunrises and day-vistas and sunsets, she passed her girlhood and bloomed into womanhood. In this old adobe building she queened it supremely. Here she presided at every hospitality; here she was the leader of every fiesta.

To this bay, on the 8th of April, 1806[11], in the absence of her stern old father in Monterey, and while the Presidio was under the temporary command of her brother Luis, there came from the north the "Juno," the vessel of the Russian Chamberlain Rezánov, his secret mission an intrigue of some kind concerning this wonderland, for the benefit of the great Czar at St. Petersburg. He found no difficulty in coming ashore. Father was away. Brother was kind. Besides, the Russian marines looked good, and the officers knew how to dance as only military men know how to dance. The hospitality was Castilian, unaffected, intimate, and at the evenings' dances in this old building their barrego was more graceful than any inartistic tango, and in the teaching of the waltz by the Russians—there was no "hesitation."

Then came Love's miracle; and by the time the comandante returned to his

---

[11] G. H. von Langsdorff, Voyages and Travels in Various Parts of the World (Henry Colburn, London, 1814), part 2, page 150. Langsdorff, of course, gives it as March 28, 1806, old style, in that year twelve days earlier than our calendar west of the 180th degree of longitude, and eleven days earlier than our calendar cast of that degree. H. H. Bancroft states that "the loss of a day in coming eastward from St. Petersburg was never taken into account until Alaska was transferred to the United States" (Bancroft, Hist. of California, II, page 299, foot-note 9). Certainly, Langsdorff makes no such allowance in his narrative of old-style dates, and in the only place east of the 180th parallel where he computes the corresponding new style he adds eleven days, instead of twelve (Voyages and Travels, II, page 136). Bancroft adopts the date of April 5th, basing it on the Tikhmenef narrative. Richman and Eldredge follow him in preferring the Tikhmenef narrative to the Langsdorff narrative as a basis, though they differ from each other in reducing it to the new style from the old style, Richman making it April 5th, following Bancroft in this regard also, and Eldredge making it April 4th, I prefer, with Father Engelhardt, to follow as a basis the painstaking German, Langsdorff, who kept his diary day by day.

post, ten days later, the glances of the bright-flashing eyes of the daughter had more effectively pulverized the original scheme of the chamberlain, than any old guns of her father on this fort could have done. Their troth was plighted, and, as he belonged to the Greek Church, with a lover's abandon, he started home to St. Petersburg, the tremendous journey of that day by way of Russian America and across the plains of Siberia, to obtain his Emperor's consent to his marriage. No knight of chivalry ever pledged more determined devotion. He assured even the Governor that, immediately upon his return to St. Petersburg, he would go to Madrid as ambassador extraordinary from the Czar, to obviate every kind of misunderstanding between the powers. From there he would proceed to Vera Cruz, or some other Spanish harbor in Mexico, and then return to San Francisco, to claim his bride.

On the 21st of May, about four o'clock in the afternoon, the "Juno" weighed anchor for Sitka, and in passing the fort, then called the fort of San Joaquin, she saluted it with seven guns—and received in return a salute of nine. The old chronicler who accompanied the expedition says that the Governor, with the whole Argüello family, and several other friends and acquaintances, collected at the fort and waived an adieu with hats and handkerchiefs[12]. And one loyal soul stood looking seaward, till a vessel's hull sank below the horizon.

How many fair women, through the pitiless years, have thus stood—looking seaward! Once more the envious Fates prevailed. Unknown to his sweetheart, Rezánov died on the overland journey from Okhotsk to St. Petersburg, in a little town in the snows of central Siberia. With a woman's instinctive and unyielding faith, the beautiful girl waited and watched for his return, waited the long and dreary years till the roses of youth faded from her cheeks. True heart, no other voice could reach her ear! Dead to all allurement, she first joined a secular order, "dedicating her life to the instructions of the young and the consolation of the sick," and finally entered the Dominican sisterhood, where she gave the remainder of her life to the heroic and self-effacing service of her order. Not until late in life did she have the consolation of learning—and then quite by accident—that her lover had not been false to her, but had died of a fall from his horse on his mission to win her. Long years afterward she died, in 1857, at the convent of St. Catherine; and today, while he sleeps beneath a Greek cross in the wilds of Siberia, she is at rest beneath a Roman cross in the little Dominican cemetery at Benicia, across the Bay[13].

[12] G. H. von Langsdorff, Voyages and Travels, part 2, pages 183, 217. Tikhmenef's narrative would make the "Juno" leave on the 19th of May, but Langsdorff was himself aboard and kept a log.

[13] Nicolaï Petróvich Rezánov, Chamberlain to the Czar, died March 13, 1807 (March 1, old style), at the little town of Krasnoïarsk, capital of the Province of Yenisseisk, now a station on the Trans-Siberian Railroad, where his body is still interred. Von Langsdorff visited his grave Dec. 9, 1807 (Nov. 27, old style), and found a tomb which be described as "a large stone, in the fashion of an altar, but without any inscription." (Voyages and Travels, part 2, page 385.) Sir George Simpson visited the grave in 1842, and states that a tomb had been erected by the Russian American Company in 1831, but does not describe it. Whether this is a mistake in the date on his part, or whether a later and more elaborate tomb displaced the first one, I have not yet been able to ascertain. It is certain, however, that

This history is true. These old walls were witnesses to part of it. These hills and dales were part of the setting for their love-drama. One picnic was taken by boat to what is now called the Island of Belvedere yonder. One horseback outing was taken to the picturesque cañon of San Andrés, so named by Captain Rivera and Father Palou in 1774. Gertrude Atherton has given us the novel, and Bret Harte has sung the poem, founded upon it[14].

When we think of the love stories that have survived the ages, Alexander and Thais, Pericles and Aspasia, Antony and Cleopatra, and all the rest of them—some of them a narrative unfit to handle with tongs—shall we let this local story die? Shall not America furnish a newer and purer standard? If to such a standard Massachusetts is to contribute the Courtship of Miles Standish, may not California contribute the Courtship of Rezánov? You men of this army post have a peculiar right to proclaim this sentiment; in such an enlistment you, of all men, would have the right to unsheathe a flaming sword. For this memory of the comandante's daughter is yours—yours to cherish, yours to protect. In the barracks and on parade, at the dance and in the field, this "one sweet human fancy" belongs to this Presidio; and no court-martial nor departmental order can ever take it from you.

Sir George Simpson had read von Langsdorff's book.

The body of Sor Dominga Argüello, commonly called Sister Mary Dominica (Concepción Argüello) after her death, which occurred Dec. 23, 1857, was first interred in the small cemetery in the convent yard, but in the latter part of 1897 (Original Annals, St. Catherine's, Benicia), when the bodies were removed, it was reinterred in the private cemetery of the Dominican order overlooking Suisun Bay, on the heights back of the old military barracks. Her grave is the innermost one, in the second row, of the group in the southwesterly corner of the cemetery. It is marked by a humble white marble slab, on which is graven a little cross with her name and the date of her death. This grave deserves to be as well known as that of Heloïse and Abelard, in the cemetery of Père Lachaise.

[14] "Rezánov," by Gertrude Atherton (John Murray, London). See also Appendix B. The quaint poem of Richard E. White to "The Little Dancing Saint" (*Overland*, May, 1914) is worthy of mention, though the place of her childhood is mistakenly assumed to be Lower California instead of San Francisco. It is to be hoped also that the very clever skit of Edward F. O'Day, entitled "The Defeat of Rezánov," purely imaginative as a historical incident, but with a wealth of local "atmosphere," written for the Family Club, of San Francisco, and produced at one of its "Farm Plays," will yet be published, and not buried in the archives of a club.

[TRANSLATION OF BAPTISMAL RECORD.]

931. Maria de la Concepción Marcela Argüello, Female Spanish Infant 65.

On the 26th day of February of the year 1791, in the church of this Mission of our Holy Patron St. Francis, I solemnly baptized a girl born on the 19th day of the said month, the legitimate daughter of Don José Argüello, lieutenant-captain, and commander of the neighboring royal presidio, a native of the city of Querétaro, New Spain, and of Doña Maria Ygnacia Moraga, a native of the royal presidio of El Altar, Sonora. I gave her the names of Maria de la Concepción Marcela. Her godfather was Don José de Zuñiga, lieutenant-captain and commander of the royal presidio of San Diego, by proxy, authenticated by the colonel commandant-inspector and Governor of this province, Señor Don Pedro Fages, in the presence of two witnesses, namely, Señor Manuel de Vargas, sergeant of the company of Monterey, and Juan de Dios Ballesteros, corporal of the same, delegated in due form to Manuel Baronda, corporal of the company of this royal presidio of our Holy Patron St. Francis, who accepted it, and held the said girl in his arms at the time of her baptism. I notified him that he was not contracting kinship nor the obligations of godfather, and that he should so advise his principal, in order that the latter might be informed of the spiritual kinship and of other obligations contracted, according as I explained them to him. And in witness whereof, I sign it on the day, mouth and year above given.

Fray Pedro Benito Cambon (rubric).

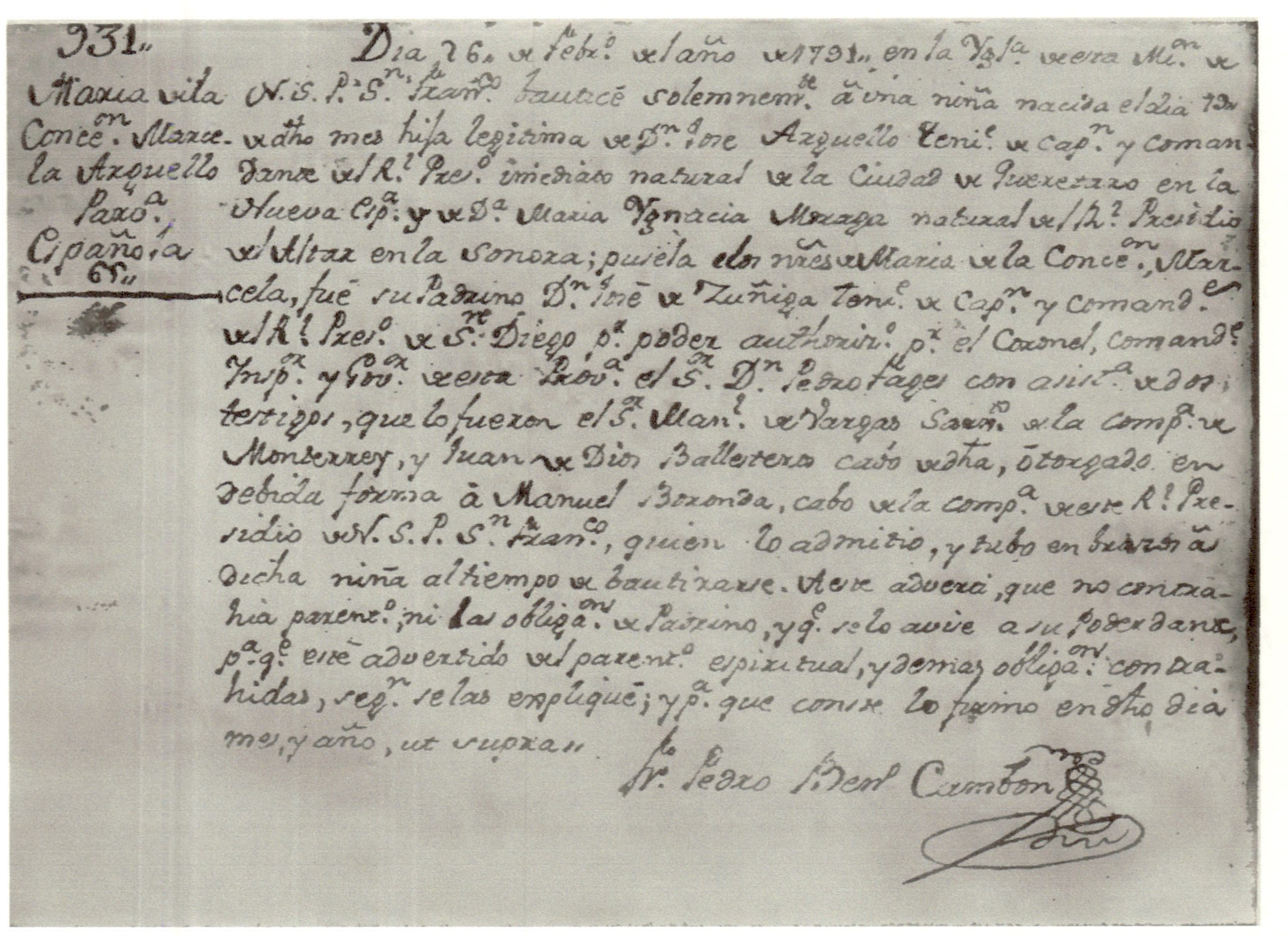

931.

María
Concepⁿ
la Arguello
Paxᵃ
Cipañola
65.

Dia 26. de feb.º del año de 1791. en la Yglª de la Missⁿ de
Maria vtia N.S.P.S. S.ⁿ Franco bauticé solemnemᵗᵉ á vna niña nacida el dia 19
de dho mes hija legitima de D.ⁿ Jose Arguello Teni.ᵉ de cap.ⁿ y coman-
te dl R.ˡ Presº imediato natural de la Ciudad de Queretaro en la
Nueva Espª y de Dª Maria Ygnacia Moraga natural del Rˡ Presidio
del Altar en la Sonora; pusela dos nres de Maria de la Conceⁿ, Marcela, fué su Padrino D.ⁿ Jose de Zuñiga teni.ᵉ de cap.ⁿ y comand.ᵉ
dl Rˡ Presº de S.ⁿ Diego p.r poder authorirº p.r el Coronel, comandᵉ
Inspᵒʳ y Govᵒʳ de la Provª el S.r D.ⁿ Pedro fages con asistᵃ de dos
testigos, que lo fueron el S.ⁿ Manˡ de Vargas Sarxᵗᵒ de la compª de
Monterrey, y Juan de Dios Ballesteros cabo dtha, otorgado en
debida forma à Manuel Boronda, cabo de la compª de este Rˡ Presidio de N.S.P. S.ⁿ Franco, quien lo admitió, y tuvo en braxᵒ á
dicha niña al tiempo de bautixarse. deve adverti, que no contra-
hia parentᵉ ni las obligaⁿ de Padrino, y gᵉ se lo avise a su poderdanᵗᵉ
p.ªqᵉ ese advertido del parentᵉ espiritual, y demas obligaⁿ contra-
hidas, segⁿ se las expliqué; y p.ª que const lo firmo en dho dia
mes, y año, ut supra.

Fr. Pedro Benᵗ Cambon

ORIGINAL RECORD OF BAPTISM OF CONCEPCIÓN ARGÜELLO

APPENDIX B.

CONCEPCIÓN DE ARGÜELLO (BRET HARTE).

(Presidio de San Francisco, 1806.)

By Bret Harte.

I.

Looking seaward, o'er the sand-hills stands the fortress, old and quaint,
By the San Francisco friars lifted to their patron saint, —

Sponsor to that wondrous city, now apostate to the creed,
On whose youthful walls the Padre saw the angel's golden reed;

All its trophies long since scattered, all its blazon brushed away;
And the flag that flies above it but a triumph of today.

Never scar of siege or battle challenges the wandering eye,
Never breach of warlike onset holds the curious passer-by;

Only one sweet human fancy interweaves its threads of gold
With the plain and homespun present, and a love that ne'er grows old;

Only one thing holds its crumbling walls above the meaner dust,
Listen to the simple story of a woman's love and trust.

II.

Count von Resanoff[15], the Russian, envoy of the mighty Czar,
Stood beside the deep embrasures, where the brazen cannon are.

He with grave provincial magnates long had held serene debate
On the Treaty of Alliance and the high affairs of state;

He from grave provincial magnates oft had turned to talk apart
With the Comandante's daughter on the questions of the heart,

Until points of gravest import yielded slowly one by one,

---

[15] If the facsimile of the chamberlain's signature, when written in Roman alphabetical character, is as set forth in part 2 of the Russian publication "Istoritcheskoé Obosrénié Obrasovania Rossiisko-Amerikanskoi Kompanii," by P. Tikhmenef, published in 1863, by Edward Weimar, in St. Petersburg, then the proper spelling is "Rezanov," the accent on the penult, and the "v" pronounced like "ff."

For metrical purposes Bret Harte has here taken the same kind of liberty with "Resanoff," and in another poem with Portolá, as Byron took with Trafálgar, in Childe Harold.

And by Love was consummated what Diplomacy begun;

Till beside the deep embrasures, where the brazen cannon are,
He received the twofold contract for approval of the Czar;

Till beside the brazen cannon the betrothèd bade adieu,
And from sallyport and gateway north the Russian eagles flew.

III.

Long beside the deep embrasures, where the brazen cannon are,
Did they wait the promised bridegroom and the answer of the Czar;

Day by day on wall and bastion beat the hollow, empty breeze,—
Day by day the sunlight glittered on the vacant, smiling seas;

Week by week the near hills whitened in their dusty leather cloaks,
Week by week the far hills darkened from the fringing plain of oaks;

Till the rains came, and far breaking, on the fierce southwester tost,
Dashed the whole long coast with color, and then vanished and were
    lost.

So each year the seasons shifted,—wet and warm and drear and dry;
Half a year of clouds and flowers, half a year of dust and sky.

Still it brought no ship nor message,—brought no tidings, ill or meet,
For the statesmanlike Commander, for the daughter fair and sweet.

Yet she heard the varying message, voiceless to all ears beside:
"He will come," the flowers whispered; "Come no more," the dry hills
    sighed.

Still she found him with the waters lifted by the morning breeze,—
Still she lost him with the folding of the great white-tented seas;

Until hollows chased the dimples from her cheeks of olive brown,
And at times a swift, shy moisture dragged the long sweet lashes down;

Or the small mouth curved and quivered as for some denied caress,
And the fair young brow was knitted in an infantine distress.

Then the grim Commander, pacing where the brazen cannon are,
Comforted the maid with proverbs, wisdom gathered from afar;

Bits of ancient observation by his fathers garnered, each
As a pebble worn and polished in the current of his speech:

"'Those who wait the coming rider travel twice as far as he;'
'Tired wench and coming butter never did in time agree;'

"'He that getteth himself honey, though a clown, he shall have flies;'
'In the end God grinds the miller;' 'In the dark the mole has eyes;'

"'He whose father is Alcalde of his trial hath no fear,'—
And be sure the Count has reasons that will make his conduct clear."

Then the voice sententious faltered, and the wisdom it would teach

Lost itself in fondest trifles of his soft Castilian speech;

And on "Concha," "Conchitita," and "Conchita" he would dwell
With the fond reiteration which the Spaniard knows so well.

So with proverbs and caresses, half in faith and half in doubt,
Every day some hope was kindled, flickered, faded, and went out.

IV.

Yearly, down the hillside sweeping, came the stately cavalcade,
Bringing revel to vaquero, joy and comfort to each maid;

Bringing days of formal visit, social feast and rustic sport,
Of bull-baiting on the plaza, of love-making in the court.

Vainly then at Concha's lattice, vainly as the idle wind,
Rose the thin high Spanish tenor that bespoke the youth too kind;

Vainly, leaning from their saddles, caballeros, bold and fleet,
Plucked for her the buried chicken from beneath their mustang's feet;

So in vain the barren hillsides with their gay serapes blazed,—
Blazed and vanished in the dust-cloud that their flying hoofs had raised.

Then the drum called from the rampart, and once more, with
     patient mien,
The Commander and his daughter each took up the dull routine,

Each took up the petty duties of a life apart and lone,
Till the slow years wrought a music in its dreary monotone.

V.

Forty years on wall and bastion swept the hollow idle breeze,
Since the Russian eagle fluttered from the California seas;

Forty years on wall and bastion wrought its slow but sure decay,
And St. George's cross was lifted in the port of Monterey;

And the citadel was lighted, and the hall was gayly drest,
All to honor Sir George Simpson, famous traveler and guest[16].

[16] The mention of Monterey is a poetic license. Sir George Simpson actually met her and acquainted her for the first time with the immediate cause of her lover's death, at Santa Barbara, where she was living with the De la Guerra family, Jan. 24, 1842, after her return from Lower California, following the death of her parents. "Though Doña Concepción," wrote Sir George Simpson, in 1847, "apparently loved to dwell on the story of her blighted affections, yet, strange to say, she knew not, till we mentioned it to her, the immediate cause of the chancellor's sudden death. This circumstance might in some measure be explained by the fact that Langsdorff's work was not published before 1814; but even then, in any other country than California, a lady who was still young, would surely have seen a book, which, besides detailing the grand incident of her life, presented so gratifying a portrait of her charms." (An Overland Journey Round the World, during the years 1841 and 1842, by Sir George Simpson, Governor-in-chief of the Hudson Bay Company's Territories, published by Lea and Blanchard, Philadelphia, in 1847, page 207.)

Far and near the people gathered to the costly banquet set,
And exchanged congratulations with the English baronet;

Till, the formal speeches ended, and amidst the laugh and wine,
Some one spoke of Concha's lover,—heedless of the warning sign.

Quickly then cried Sir George Simpson: "Speak no ill of him, I pray!
He is dead. He died, poor fellow, forty years ago this day,

"Died while speeding home to Russia, falling from a fractious horse.
Left a sweetheart, too, they tell me. Married, I suppose, of course!

"Lives she yet?" A deathlike silence fell on banquet, guests, and hall,
And a trembling figure rising fixed the awestruck gaze of all.

Two black eyes in darkened orbits gleamed beneath the nun's white
        hood[17];
Black serge hid the wasted figure, bowed and stricken where it stood.

"Lives she yet?" Sir George repeated. All were hushed as Concha drew
Closer yet her nun's attire. "Señor, pardon, she died, too!"

---

[17] She did not actually receive the white habit till she was received into the Dominican sisterhood, April 11, 1851, by Padre F. Sadoc Vilarrasa, in the Convent of Santa Catalina
de Sena (St. Catherine of Siena), at Monterey, being the first one to enter, where she took the
perpetual vow April 13, 1852 (Original Records, Book of Clothings and Professions, page
1, now at Dominican College, at San Rafael, Cal.), and where she remained continuously
till the convent was transferred to Benicia, Aug. 26, 1854. There being no religious order for
women in California until the Dominican sisterhood was founded at Monterey, March 13,
1851 (Original Annals, at Benicia, Reg. 1, pages I and 14), she had at first to content herself
with joining the Third Order of St. Francis "in the world," and it was really the dark habit
of this secular order which constituted the "nun's attire" at the time Sir George Simpson
met her in 1842.

Lector House believes that a society develops through a two-fold approach of continuous learning and adaptation, which is derived from the study of classic literary works spread across the historic timeline of literature records. Therefore, we aim at reviving, repairing and redeveloping all those inaccessible or damaged but historically as well as culturally important literature across subjects so that the future generations may have an opportunity to study and learn from past works to embark upon a journey of creating a better future.

This book is a result of an effort made by Lector House towards making a contribution to the preservation and repair of original ancient works which might hold historical significance to the approach of continuous learning across subjects.

HAPPY READING & LEARNING!

LECTOR HOUSE LLP
E-MAIL: info@lectorhouse.com